Seven Last Words

"The words that you gave to me
I have given to them, and they have
received them and know in truth
that I came from you."
–John 17:8

SEVEN LAST WORDS

Lenten Reflections for Today's Believers

ALICE CAMILLE

ASSISTING CHRISTIANS TO ACT
PUBLICATIONS

Seven Last Words
Lenten Reflections for Today's Believers
by Alice Camille

Cover Design by Tom A. Wright
Edited and typeset by Patrice J. Tuohy

Scripture quotations are from the *New Revised Standard Version* of the Bible, copyright © 1989, Division of Christian Education of the National Council of the Churches of Christ in the United States of America. Used with permission. All rights reserved.

Copyright © 1998 by Alice Camille

Published by ACTA Publications
4848 North Clark Street
Chicago, IL 60640
800-397-2282

Library of Congress Catolog Number: 98-73096
ISBN: 0-87946-191-8
Printed in the United States of America
02 01 00 99 98 5 4 3 2 1 First Printing

Contents

For GREG APPARCEL,
who first let me preach and believed in my vocation.

Introduction

THE FINAL WORDS of a dying person are precious to those left behind. When time is short, one has a chance to speak only of the most important things—love, forgiveness, faith. The last words are often the summation of a life, cherished and pondered long after the loved one has died. The final testament of a human life can be known in these words.

That is why the church has a long tradition of meditating on the last words of Jesus from the cross. What are those words? The answer is not so simple. The story of the crucifixion as we know it is really four stories, preserved in the unique accounts of the Evangelists. Both Mark and Matthew record that Jesus spoke only once from the cross, saying, *My God, my God, why have you forsaken me?* This quote from Psalm 22, often seen as a cry of despair, is actually a prayer of confidence in the midst of anguish, as the psalmist intended.

But in the gospels of Luke and John, Jesus does not speak these words. In these gospels, Jesus speaks three times from the cross, and the three sayings are not the same. According to Luke, Jesus speaks about forgiveness and confident surrender to God. This is consistent with Luke's overall presentation of Jesus as a gentle pastor, a man of compassion and obedience.

In John's gospel, Jesus is always in charge of his destiny—the Lord of History, marching resolutely to the cross. In keeping with that powerful portrayal, Jesus speaks as a man settling his accounts in the end. He commends his mother to the care of his friend. He speaks to fulfill the scripture. And he concludes with the words of triumph: *It is finished!*

From the first centuries, the church has seen a value in these collective accounts of the story of Jesus. There were, as we know, many more than four versions of the gospel written in the early centuries, and of these only four were chosen as authentically inspired for use in the canon of scripture. A movement to narrow the gospel to one account was made in the second century, but the Church Fathers decided that these four testimonies contributed to the story in ways too vital to lose.

And so the blending of these seven last sayings of Jesus from all four gospels became part of the church's Lenten tradition. The ordering of the Seven Words, as they are called, has been standardized over the centuries, although this is not necessarily a historical sequence, any more than the Stations of the Cross can be said to be strictly historical. In this way the Seven Words have been set to music, used in sacred dramas, and pondered in Good Friday observances in churches around the world. In our own time, beloved Bishop Fulton Sheen, theologian Karl Rahner, and Pope John Paul II have all published meditations on the Seven Last Words of Christ. In this last testament of Jesus, all Christians find a pearl of great price.

THE FIRST WORD

Father, forgive them;
for they do not know what they are doing.

THE FIRST WORD

When they came to the place that is called The Skull, they crucified Jesus there with the criminals, one on his right and one on his left. Then Jesus said, "FATHER, FORGIVE THEM; FOR THEY DO NOT KNOW WHAT THEY ARE DOING" (Luke 23:33-34).

HUMILITY

A FRIEND has betrayed him. His own religious leaders have handed him over to the enemy, and he has been condemned to death. One of his closest companions has denied he even knows him. His longtime disciples have deserted him. Strangers drive nails into his body, and crowds who do not care about his love or his Father are making a joke of his suffering.

And Jesus forgives them all. Forgives Judas and the High Priest and Pilate and Peter. He forgives the followers who had no courage, the soldiers who perform the crucifixion, and the people who seek to humiliate him in the very act of their ridicule. Jesus does not wait for them to say they are sorry, to come to him with contrition, to prove they have changed. He asks his Father's forgiveness for them even as they are putting him to death, even though no one shows a hint of remorse.

This is such a staggering, unheard of, inconceivable act of forgiveness that it is easy to overlook the rest of what Jesus says. We are lost in a place between awe and horror at the nobility of one who forgives in this way. We feel awe at the largeness of such a spirit and horror that we may be asked to do the same, to forgive with such generosity. We feel sure that we can't. It is hard enough to forgive those who regret the injury they have caused. To forgive those who do not seek our forgiveness or show concern for our suffering seems to be asking too much.

To follow the example of Jesus, we have to hear *all* of what he says. First of all, he does not say, "I forgive you." He says, *Father, forgive them.* What we in our humanity cannot dream of doing, God in full divinity can and will. We can pray for God's forgiveness of our enemies. We can ask God to go beyond the limitations of the human heart and do what God does best: forgive a sinful creation.

This is an important lesson to learn from Jesus because the culture in which we live tells a much different story. The ancient code of an eye for an eye is very much alive and well. If people cause harm, people ought to pay. Restitution may be a form of justice, but the forgiveness Jesus teaches goes beyond justice to the new covenant of mercy. If God exacted from us pure justice, no one would be saved, as the disciples once fearfully understood. But the forgiveness Jesus preached and offered, to the last hour on the cross, requires no eye-for-an-eye restitution. It is God's free gift. It can't be bought or earned or deserved.

We don't need to wait for restoration to forgive those

who wrong us. We don't have to wait for healing to come or for our emotions to catch up to our Christian duty. We can ask God to forgive our enemies *for* us, as Jesus did. Only then can real healing begin. For when we hold no one bound who sins against us, neither are we held bound by the desire for vengeance.

Father, forgive them. It is a staggering proposition, but the reason Jesus offers is even more stunning: *they do not know what they are doing.* What gets sinners off the hook is not our goodness, our contrition, our well-meaning intentions, or our pledge to do better. It is our ignorance that makes us eligible for forgiveness. A truly humbling thought!

The creation story in Genesis sheds light on this mystery. The Evil One uses knowledge as a temptation: "You will be like God, knowing good and evil." And, in fact, the eyes of the first couple are opened and they do come out of innocence into a kind of knowledge. But knowledge without wisdom is hopelessly crippled. They see, but they do not understand. And their actions betray their ignorance.

The seven capital sins are all rooted in this original ignorance. We are proud, because we do not see how small and fallible we are. We are greedy because we think things can bring us happiness. We are lazy because we have grain enough stored in the barn for tomorrow—forgetting that tomorrow may not come. We envy others, not seeing how jealousy poisons our ability to love. We harbor anger and forget the mandate to seek reconciliation. We see others through the prism of lust and distort them into mere objects for our own satisfaction. We approach food or drink or other pleasures gluttonously, forgetting our responsibility to those who do not have what they need to survive.

All of those responsible for the crucifixion acted out of a destructive ignorance. Judas didn't believe Jesus was the Messiah of God, and fear blinded Peter's faith. Caiaphas could only see as far as the boundary of his authority, which was threatened by the teachings of this rabbi. Pilate had a similar blind spot beyond his own jurisdiction. The soldiers were just following orders. The crowds were following custom. Everybody had an excuse for how they acted, and all of them did not know what they were doing, and to whom.

The knowledge that we are sinners is not to make us feel hateful but to know how loved we are.

So what is the answer to original ignorance? The virtue of humility. Saint Bernard of Clairvaux said it simply: "There are only four virtues: humility, humility, humility, and humility." In the presence of this great virtue, pride gets down on its knees. Greed opens its hands. Sloth tends to its responsibilities. Envy looks away from its neighbor. Anger forgets its grudge. Lust remembers the person behind the obsession and is stilled. Gluttony puts down its fork and extends its plate to someone else. Humility resolves all conflict, forgives every enemy, and lives in peace with everyone.

Humility makes us wince because it sounds like

humiliation, and no one wants to be humiliated. Others tried to humiliate Jesus on the cross. He showed them humility in return. In humiliation there is shame, but in humility, great dignity. Humiliation comes when someone is brought low. Humility is when one bends low for the sake of others. As Saint Paul wrote in his letter to the Philippians:

> Though he was in the form of God,
> > [Jesus] did not deem equality with God
> > as something to be exploited,
> but emptied himself,
> > taking the form of a slave
> > being born in human likeness.
> And being found in human form,
> > he humbled himself
> > and became obedient to the point of death–
> > even death on a cross.

This kind of behavior can't be found much because it does not seek to be discovered. Do not trust anyone who says, "I am humble." The wearer of the humble pin is automatically disqualified by definition from wearing it.

Humility must be practiced in private. Recognition that we are all sinners is the foundation of this virtue. Even Jesus did not deem equality with God something to be clung to–yet it is amazing how many churchgoing people act as if that is the goal of religion. In a Catholic celebration of the Eucharist, a priest once gave this call at communion time: "This table is set for sinners! May the sinners come forward; the righteous can all go home." Not a soul in the church was deterred from receiving the sacrament by this summons. True humility is knowing who we really are. We are sinners, and Christ didn't die for anyone else.

Some people have grown tired of feel-bad religion, the kind that makes them languish in guilt and feel paralyzed in attempts to do better. The knowledge that we are sinners is not to make us feel hateful but to know how loved we are. Being sinners, we can abandon the game of pretending we are perfect. Being sinners ourselves, we find it easier to forgive others. Being sinners, we know there is much we don't know, and that is a great relief. We can lay down the burden of trying to save ourselves by our righteousness and let God do the saving.

People who know that God saves are said to be born again. Jesus invites us to start over in just this image. When Jesus said we have to become like little children to follow him to the Kingdom, he didn't mean for us to get cute and cuddly or to become innocent again. No one born into original sin can find the way back to a pre-sinful state. But children are eager to learn, and in their natural humility they know there is much to learn. To become like children, we have to abandon the adult premise that we know it all and sit at the feet of the Teacher again.

This goes against everything our culture tells us about what it means to be a successful person. Successful people are supposed to have all the answers, believe in their own personal power, and control their own destinies. To say "I don't know" is to betray weakness, and that is a big mistake. To ask "Teach me" is to lose the position of superiority over another. To say "I was wrong"

is to prove mortality, which simply means we know we
are not God.

The psychologist Rollo May offered this axiom for
truly successful living: "I am human, therefore limited,
therefore imperfect, therefore disappointing to myself and
others." This is not negative self-talk; this is a reality
check! This might not make a bad addition to one's
evening prayer practice, an hour the church has always
recommended for reflection and reconciliation. At the
end of the day, we see all the ways we took shortcuts with
integrity, preferring expedience to kindness, the selfish
motive to the generous, judgment to the compassionate
response.

Saint Philip Neri prayed this prayer every day: "Lord,
watch Philip: he will betray you!" What our culture might
dismiss as a poor self-image on Philip's part, we can see
in the light of faith as a clear-eyed view of the truth about
ourselves. No one of us is beyond the temptation to look
out for Number One by telling little white lies, gossiping
to bring others down, or being silent in the face of
injustice. Just as we seek Christ in those who are suffering, we can also see the contents of our own hearts
mirrored in the most wretched of sinners. "There, but for
God's grace, go I." The humble person understands that
no human life is so very different from any other, no
matter how extreme the events that shape each one.

The great danger for the so-called good person is to
think that he or she cannot sin or cannot descend as far
into sin as others have. "I could never murder," a man
says to himself. "I could never commit adultery," a woman
insists. The Evil One is tempted by such challenges to the

real power of sin, and such ignorance can bring a person
to ruin. The holy person, with the wisdom reaped in
humility, will only say, "Lord, preserve me from the near
occasion of this sin."

We do not know what we are doing. We think we are
clever, self-possessed, and have a greater degree of self-
knowledge than others, perhaps because we pray,
meditate, or take days for recollection and retreat. But
the human will to get more than what we already have
nests in every heart like a cobra waiting to assert itself.

Theologians call this concupiscence, or desire, which is the
fatal effect of original sin. We humans are not satisfied even in
Paradise but are ever seeking more. That part of us that is made for eternity
yearns to express its likeness to divinity in ways that
eclipse our obedience to God. Instead of seeking God, we
seek ourselves and serve the wrong master.

> *Humility won't make us sinless, but it will make us repent. It's a matter of direction, not perfection.*

Humility won't make us sinless, but it will make us
repent. It's a matter of direction, not perfection. Imagine a
room in which God is at the center and two people are in
the Divine Presence. One person kneels at the foot of
God and another stands at the door, one hand turning
the knob. Which person is closer to God?

Western tradition would lead us to guess at once
that the person right next to God is closer. But in the

Buddhist tradition, the answer would depend on the direction each person was facing. The person kneeling at the foot of God may be turned away, while the person at the door may be glancing back, eager to return. If a person is close to God but moving away, he or she will never reach the Divine Presence. But a person turned to God, no matter how far away, will come into the embrace of God in time.

Jesus asked his Father to forgive his betrayers and tormentors because of their ignorance. Humility is the virtue of knowing we possess a frail and partial knowledge of the ways of good and evil. Humility leads us to become like little children, to seek wisdom at the foot of the cross. As Saint Paul tells us, "Now we see as in a mirror, dimly. But then we will see face to face."

THE SECOND WORD

*Truly I tell you,
today you will be with me
in Paradise.*

THE SECOND WORD

One of the criminals who were hanged there kept deriding him and saying, "Are you not the Messiah? Save yourself and us!" But the other rebuked him saying, "Do you not fear God, since you are under the same sentence of condemnation? And we indeed have been condemned justly, for we are getting what we deserve for our deeds, but this man has done nothing wrong." Then he said, "Jesus, remember me when you come into your kingdom."

He replied, "TRULY I TELL YOU, TODAY YOU WILL BE WITH ME IN PARADISE" (Luke 23:39-43).

THE KINGDOM

WHO WAS this man tradition calls the good thief? He has neither name nor history, only the promise of an everlasting future of joy. His anonymity is like that of so many who stepped out of the shadows of Judea to be healed, forgiven, and transformed by Jesus. Out of the depths of their humanity, their suffering, their ordinariness, they rose up to encounter him. And each in turn was invited to share in the good news of the reign of God.

The good thief is one such footnote in the gospels.

He and his companion are not technically thieves at all; both are called insurgents or revolutionaries. This is the same word used to describe the occupation of Barabbas, the man whose life was traded for Christ's. All three men were, ironically, guilty of the charge for which Jesus is innocently crucified, which is treason.

Was the good thief a Zealot, like Simon who followed Jesus? The majority of Judeans at that time were peasants who suffered the taxation of both the Romans and the Temple and had little love for authority of any kind. Some became revolutionaries for religious reasons, and some for economic ones. Some joined bandit gangs in Robin Hood style to take from the rich and give to the poor, who happened to be themselves. Some joined bands of "daggermen," who performed assassinations on religious leaders. They were protesting the betrayal they felt by those who collaborated with the Romans to remain in power.

The gospels paint a pastoral picture of Jesus preaching serenely through the countryside, while sheep graze just beyond the crowds. In fact, the first century was seething with political unrest, social chaos, and mayhem. The soldiers of the occupation swept into towns and murdered citizens without warning, while Jews murdered their own countrymen in disillusionment. Religious fanatics and homegrown militias and occasional prophets mobilized local citizens to fight for liberation. So-called messiahs were raised up and put to death by the dozens in the century before Jesus.

The Romans did not distinguish between the bandits, prophets, and self-proclaimed messiahs but

crucified them all routinely. So there is no way of knowing whether the good thief was a poor man who had the
misfortune to travel once with a bandit gang or whether
he was a career assassin.

What is clear is that the two men in Luke's portrayal
of this scene are not the same, even though they bear the
same sentence for the same crime. Mark and Matthew
tell the story differently from Luke. In their versions, both
criminals take part in mocking Jesus, and there is no
distinction drawn between the two. But Luke is ever the
gospel of the second chance, and so we are shown this
moment of decision, in which one man departs from the
popular path to follow Jesus.

Throughout the Gospel of Luke, Jesus has been
seeking faith in his listeners, wondering whether, when
the Son of Man returns, he will find faith at all. The signs
of faith are rare among the religious but surprisingly
fertile among the unlikely: sinners, the sick, and Gentiles.
Jesus sought long and hard for faith among the crowds
who followed him in his glory hours while he taught
brilliantly, healed the sick, and challenged authority
publicly. Those who shared in his private hour of Transfiguration saw his glory revealed in full—and yet they are
absent in his hour of desolation. All those who sided with
him during the glory days are gone.

And now, when Jesus has never looked less a king,
when glory is obscured by bruises, a poor dying criminal
makes an act of faith! This one sees no miracle, hears no
remarkable wisdom; he views only the agonized body of a
fellow sufferer, close to certain death. There is nothing
wonderful at the cross to prompt a creed, and yet this

man speaks to Jesus of his Kingdom with such reverence.
This is the greatest testimony of faith in the gospels. And
in response to it, Jesus promises him the Kingdom. To
the one who can see the face of God in a crucified man,
the gates of Paradise are open.

The Kingdom of God is like a mustard seed that
Jesus carries in his pocket all the while he is ministering.
He looks for a speck of faith to bury it in, to let it come
to full flower. When the sick and desperate come to him
and profess their faith and ask his help, Jesus declares
over and over, "Your faith has saved you." Just as the faith of
the good thief saved him. The Kingdom begins in the smallest grain of faith.

> *To the one who can see the face of God in a crucified man, the gates of Paradise are open.*

We used to hear a lot about heaven, a floating
country of souls that exists above earth and beyond pain.
It was described as the place where good people go, bad
people retiring to a more southern address. But Jesus
does not talk about such a place. His proclamation of the
Kingdom is a substantial, imminent reality that is less a
place and more an event. Jesus did not teach his disciples to pray "Let us go to heaven when we die" but
rather "May your Kingdom come." *Come*–come here? Is
the Kingdom heading our way?

To understand what we're praying for in the Lord's
Prayer, we can look to the sayings of Jesus about the
Kingdom. It's not described as a reward for good people

at all. Jesus says prostitutes, tax collectors, and sinners are getting in, and religious, respectable people are finding a door shut ahead of them. This is going to be very disappointing for many people who have been saving up good deeds and years of clean living as collateral. This doesn't sound very fair, to be honest. Shouldn't God be at least as fair as we are?

On second thought, thank God that divine justice in no way resembles ours! The only chance we have is that God has promised to cut corners for the sake of our redemption. *Redemption* literally means the process of buying back something that has been pawned for ready cash. Humanity is in hock up to its ears with the wages of sin. The only way out is to declare moral bankruptcy and let God redeem us for the Kingdom. That's why it's easier for self-acknowledging sinners to get in than proper people. Big sinners are the first ones to tell you they are no paragons of virtue and need all the help they can get.

So once we manage to attain the Kingdom, what is it we are getting?

Jesus never says, "The Kingdom is thus." He only says, "The Kingdom is like thus," and goes on to tell a little story. In Matthew's gospel alone Jesus mentions the Kingdom nearly 50 times, and never describes it the same way twice. It's a merchant of pearls, a man who buys a field, a woman baking bread, a dragnet cast into the sea. It's a mustard seed, a lost coin, a father forgiving a useless son. It's at hand, among us, within our grasp at all times. And most often, it's a meal.

We Christians listen up when the story of a meal is introduced. We think at once of the great meal we share in the Eucharist. When we eat the bread and drink the cup, we witness to the death of Jesus until he comes. The words of the Memorial Acclamation are buried deep within us. When we share the Eucharist, we remember that the one who died is the One Who Lives, and he will come again to bring life that has no end.

The Kingdom, too, is coming. The Kingdom is the life of Christ promised to the criminal on the cross—and to all who share his faith that the face of God can be seen in a crucified man. The Kingdom is Paradise, a reference to the perfect creation that God intended and will bring about again "when Christ is all in all," as Saint Paul says.

But the church understands that the Kingdom isn't just an event that will come, but is Kingdom Coming as well. It is Kingdom Arriving all the time. It is at hand, in the words of Jesus. We can touch it and know it right now.

This might seem like so much theology except for the Lord's Prayer, in which Jesus teaches his disciples to pray:

> Your Kingdom come;
> Your will be done
>   on earth as it is in heaven.

The Kingdom does come whenever God's will is done on earth as in heaven. If we want to solve the mystery of the Kingdom, all we need do is choose God's will over our own. The sublime experience of being in the presence of God, heaven itself, is known in the act of doing God's will.

The Kingdom, we can now understand, is very much among us. It is in the fidelity of those who have loved long and well. It is in the heroism of justice seekers, who stand for what is right when it is unpopular and even dangerous. It is in the peacemakers, those who refuse to enjoy the self-righteous posture of bitterness. It is manifest in those who have a heart for the poor.

Being able to see the face of God in the darkest corners of the world is to see with the eyes of the Kingdom. In the final judgment scene in Matthew, Jesus separates sheep from goats on the basis of this Kingdom-sightedness. In every misfortune, Jesus is present, and if we do not respond with compassion and generosity, we will not be possessed by the Kingdom. We cannot plead, "Lord, we didn't know it was you." The Crucified One reveals the face of God; we cannot pretend not to see.

The other criminal taunts Jesus from his own cross: "Are you not the Messiah? Save yourself and us!" How frighteningly near to some of our own prayers this sounds. When we are hurting–imprisoned by illness, loneliness, or failure–we doubt that God cares much from the lofty outreaches of a better world. We look at the cross and wonder why God permitted such suffering, and we find in this image the confirmation of our fears. God won't save. God didn't spare the Divine Son. What chance have we got?

The mystery of human suffering is explored in depth in the Book of Job, and in it we find no real answers. All of the theories about suffering advanced by religion are proposed and rejected in Job. What becomes clear at the end of the book, when God speaks out of the Whirlwind, is that human understanding is painfully limited, and nothing is beyond God's power.

Without Kingdom eyes, we experience the overwhelming disillusionment of Job. Without Kingdom eyes, we can only see the cross and our own predicament, and the misery is unbearable. The criminal who mocks is like Judas who betrayed, the high priest who denounced, and all those who saw only the man Jesus and their own fortunes rising or falling with his. Those who deserted Jesus found the cross to be a stumbling block to further belief in him. Without the sight granted to those who live the Kingdom, no one saw or suspected the resurrection.

*T*he Kingdom does come whenever God's will is done on earth as in heaven. If we want to solve the mystery of the Kingdom, all we need do is choose God's will over our own.

No one, that is, except the good thief. Because of something he heard, or something he observed in Jesus, he was able to suspect the Kingdom. Perhaps one day, before he was arrested, he had stood in a crowd when Jesus was preaching, and a word took root in him. Perhaps he knew someone who had been healed, or had seen a miracle once with his own eyes. Maybe all he knew of Jesus was the hearsay of the prison. But whatever it was, he was the only one who looked into that bloodstained face and saw all the way to heaven.

"Jesus, remember me when you come into your kingdom." That was all he offered, a simple creed, sputtered from parched lips and lungs short on air. He could have made his last words a blasphemy, like the other man. He could have taken the advice of Job's wife: "Curse God, and die." But he took the little life left in him and made it into a prayer. And for this, he inherited the fullness of God's promises.

THE THIRD WORD

Woman, here is your son.
Here is your mother.

THE THIRD WORD

When Jesus saw his mother and the disciple whom he loved standing beside her, he said to his mother, "WOMAN, HERE IS YOUR SON." Then he said to the disciple, "HERE IS YOUR MOTHER" (John 19:26-27).

DISCIPLESHIP

THE SCENE is at once stark and intimate, the group of figures silhouetted against the darkening sky. The Galilean women support each other; one male disciple stands by helplessly. Three crosses dominate the scene, bearing three dying men. In John's account alone, a few remain close to Jesus at the foot of the cross as he dies. In all of the other stories, even the women watch from a distance.

And yet it is not only the closeness of the group at the cross that makes this scene unique. Something very peculiar emerges in the Gospel of John. It was the last of the four accounts written, and unlike the other three, it is less concerned with what Jesus did and more concerned with what disciples must do. The Gospel of John sets a bare stage, and the urgency of the call to discipleship is played out upon it. The style of the writing suggests a Greek drama. The writer of John is up to something.

We sense this in the strangely stylized words of Jesus from the cross. "Woman, here is your son," he says to his mother. This saying echoes the only other appearance of Mary in this gospel, at the wedding feast of Cana. On that occasion, he also calls her "woman," a polite form of address in that society, but not warm or familial. In fact, in John's gospel, Mary's name is never mentioned at all. She is "the mother of Jesus" to the narrator, and "woman" to Jesus. We feel the sterility of the address from the distance of 2,000 years.

We ourselves have grown used to a softer relationship with the Mother of God. In our hymns, prayers, and portraits of Mary, she is a compassionate woman, a tender mother, the maternal face of the divine. We see her most frequently in relation to her son, holding up her baby with great love and gentleness. We see her also in Michelangelo's Pietà, that portrayal of heartbreak, in which she embraces the body of her dead son with a sorrow so quiet and deep as to shatter the coolest observer.

She holds the baby and the man with the same tireless, loving arms. In Michelangelo's image of bereavement, she scarcely seems to have aged, as if it were only yesterday that her son was a child playing on the streets of Nazareth. She might be saying, "How can this be?" as she once asked of Gabriel at the Annunciation. How can her son be dead so soon? How can such an extraordinary life be crushed out with such malice and misunderstanding? In the Pietà, she and her son appear to be the same age, as if time is frozen. The mother and the son are no longer seen within history but in the eternity beyond

time, which is God's reign. Mary is portrayed as dispro-
portionately large in relation to the body of her son, as if
she has already assumed the everlasting role of Mother of
All Sorrows, the one to whom the sword of anguish was
foretold.

Woman, here is your son. She holds her dead son in
silence, knowing the speechless pain of all parents who
have outlived their children, a thing contrary to nature.
The Pietà is an instinctive study of an intimate moment
of grief and a universal expression of the role of Mary for
the world.

But it is not, strictly speaking, a scriptural event. We
can presume Mary begged to hold Jesus when he was
lowered from the cross, but scripture does not say so.
Metaphorically, we have replaced the detached scene in
John with the moving image of the Pietà because this, it
seems, expresses the proper application of the words:
Here is your son.

So what is going on in John's gospel, beneath the
economy of his strange detachment? The first thing we
hear is the echo of a cadence in the words of Jesus with
an earlier phrase of Pontius Pilate: "Here is the man!"
Remember, John is using a very self-conscious literary
form, so he has planted these echoes deliberately. The
entire gospel is written in a tight structure of signs and
motifs, some of which are muted in translation but can
be discerned through careful reading. Like the reference
to Mary as "woman," Pilate displays Jesus simply as "the
man," and a wretched figure he must have appeared,
recently beaten, bearing the crown of thorns, and cloaked
in purple. He is called generically *the man*, dismissed as a

nobody, yet the crown and cloak suggest kingship, the charge made against him.

The prophet Isaiah seemed to predict this scene in the last of his four servant songs:

> See, my servant shall prosper;
>> he shall be exalted and lifted up,
>> and shall be very high.
>
> Just as there were many who were
>>> astonished at him
>>> −so marred was his appearance
>>> beyond human semblance,
>> and his form beyond that of mortals−
> So shall he startle many nations,
>> kings shall shut their mouths
>>> because of him;
> For that which had not been told them
>> they shall see,
>> and that which they had not heard
>> they shall contemplate.

Through the prophecy of Isaiah echoed in John, we understand the ironic meaning in Pilate's mocking words, "Here is the man!" Though Pilate may not mean to, he is presenting not just a man but the Son of Man, not just a costumed king but the one whose Kingdom is not of this world and will last for all ages.

Part of the puzzle of John's aloofness is solved here: the reference to Mary as *woman* has a double meaning. She is the mother of Jesus, but she also represents more than herself in this gospel. As she appears only twice, at the start of Jesus' ministry and at the cross, she becomes an emblem for both his birthing into public life at Cana, and the close of his earthly responsibilities at Golgotha.

Woman, here is your son. Here is your mother. There is a reciprocal surrender and acceptance here that is very telling. Jesus commends his mother and his disciple to each other. And who is the disciple? If you guessed John, that is only because tradition has called him John. As elsewhere in this gospel, this figure is only referred to as "the disciple whom Jesus loved." He is never given a name.

As frustrating as it may seem, what the Gospel of John presents in this scene is a son called *the man*, a mother called *woman*, and a disciple called *the one whom Jesus loved.* The Evangelist knows their names and could use them, but he chooses not to. Why would he make such a compelling scene deliberately remote?

For one thing, there is the existence of three other gospel accounts that tell the story of Jesus' life and death and resurrection, so another such account is not needed. The three other gospels, called Synoptics (which means "the same"), use the same root stories and relate them in a parallel manner at least 50 percent of the time. The writer of John's gospel is aware of that tradition and sees

> *In John's gospel, the beloved disciple has no name because we are the beloved disciple. We are to read ourselves into the plot, find our lines, and understand our destiny.*

no reason to compete with it. Ninety percent of the material in John is unique to John's telling of the story. This is not because John disagrees with the Synoptic gospels but because his story presumes them and is meant to go beyond them.

As the last author of the gospels, the fourth Evangelist also has had the advantage of time. He has had more than a generation to consider the impact and meaning of the gospel, and he writes from the cosmic perspective of a community with much time for theological reflection. Mark and Matthew may have seen Jesus as the promised Messiah of Israel, and Luke may have understood him as the new Adam, but John is the only one to call him the Word who was with God from before time, present at the creation of the world!

And in the framework of this cosmic perspective, John writes a drama that has room for eternity, divinity, humanity, and each one of us. In John's gospel, the beloved disciple has no name because *we* are the beloved disciple. We are to read ourselves into the plot, find our lines, and understand our destiny.

Knowing this, we can glance toward the hill at Golgotha and see the stage set in silhouette, those three darkened figures outlining not only an intimate and singular moment in history but a universal moment for anyone who has ever accepted the invitation: "Come, follow me." The figures of the mother and the disciple are not just historical characters but also symbols identified in many ways. The two may represent the reconciliation of Jewish and Gentile Christians, literally "Here is your Gentile son, the offspring of your faith," and "Here is the

Hebrew mother, to whom you are indebted for your salvation."

Others have pointed to a larger reunion of Israel and the Christian community, the kind of interfaith dialogue the church did not know for nearly 20 centuries until our time. Or perhaps Mary can be seen in her traditional role as the church, the mother of all Christians. Each of us is given to the church for her nurture and are given the church to defend and sustain.

In a very real way, each of us is given to one another as family, and we are represented in the shadow of the cross. We stand there, in the incredible immediacy of John's vision, and know ourselves to be flesh and bone, a part of one another's journey. "Am I my brother's keeper?" Cain once asked rhetorically. The answer that comes back to him over the years is yes; we are all responsible for one another's welfare. As the Body of Christ, we know we are in need of one another, hand unable to do without eye, all parts working together in Paul's beautiful metaphor.

Someone once approached Jesus to tell him that his family was standing at the door where he was teaching, wanting to have a word with him. Jesus answered, "Whoever does the will of my Father in heaven is my brother and sister and mother." Kinship in Christ is not about natural lineage and affinities but about sharing the body and blood of the new covenant. If we obeyed only the laws of lineage, we would be the keepers of a handful of people. Our responsibility would end with our children, or our parents, or a few other aging relations. We wouldn't have to think about the world's children, the plight of the elderly, or people of other cities, races, creeds, or customs. We could remain silent when we see a youngster illegally being sold a pack of cigarettes in a convenience store. We could look away when votes are cast against housing for the underprivileged. We could pretend it's not our business when the homeless are imprisoned for the crime of being poor, as they essentially are in some cities today.

We are very much the keepers of our brothers and sisters. We will be answerable for our actions and omissions in regard to them. *Here is your son. Here is your mother.* John invites us into a way of seeing others that is very personal and very binding on us. We are family at the foot of the cross. We are given to one another to nurture and protect. The old man needing help onto the bus is our father. The child being cruised by drug pushers at the playground is our child. The young woman applying for a job in our office is our sister. We cannot ignore or exploit the people who come into our lives, because we are disciples at the foot of the cross and each person we meet is part of our family.

> *We cannot ignore or exploit the people who come into our lives, because we are disciples at the foot of the cross and each person we meet is part of our family.*

Societies have always preferred to live by the rules of insiders and outsiders. Love your neighbor. Hate your enemy. Love your country. Hate foreigners. Care for your family. Let strangers fend for themselves. These are the tough, practical, and mostly unspoken rules of the world. They are useless to us as disciples of Jesus. We have been taught by the man on the cross to love God, love our neighbor, and love our enemy. We have been taught to see that our enemy is also our neighbor and that God's face can be seen in the need of a stranger. God, neighbor, and enemy are one in the eyes of the Kingdom. We serve God in our embrace of all three, and we deny God if we deny any one of these.

Here is your son. Here is your mother. We can flip through the pages of any news magazine and see the faces of triumph and suffering that compose our human family. We can study the faces of people on the street and see the ones who are given to us as brothers and sisters. A good meditation for discipleship is to watch a news program or sit on a city bus and say, with the appearance of each new face, "My father. My sister. My child. My family." When we encounter the face we cannot love, we must pray because that is the one who needs our love the most.

THE FOURTH WORD

My God, my God,
why have you forsaken me?

THE FOURTH WORD

*And about three o'clock, Jesus cried with a loud voice,
"Eli, Eli, lema sabachthani?" that is, "MY GOD, MY GOD,
WHY HAVE YOU FORSAKEN ME?" (Matt. 27:46).*

SUFFERING

ALL OF RELIGION is intended to answer the
question that Jesus asks so plaintively from
the cross. Philosophers and theologians frame
it differently, but it comes down to the same thing: "Why
must we suffer?" Unless it responds to this heartfelt
question convincingly and powerfully, no spirituality will
find a following.

If God is the source of all goodness and love, then
the descent into suffering seems to be in the absence of
God. If God is all-holy, then holiness and wholeness
come from God and sickness and sin must come from
some other place or being. The challenges that suffering
presents to faith are reasonable and real. Many people of
faith have stumbled on the challenge of suffering and
faltered—even abandoned faith altogether. And they might
argue that God abandoned them first.

Why do we fall sick? Why do natural disasters occur?
Why does random evil harm innocent people? Why must

we die? These questions haunt our lives and disturb our peace. When we see the suffering of others or feel great loss ourselves, we know how powerless we are, with our empty hands that cannot save.

Because the problem of suffering is so compelling for us, many schools of thought and theology have grown up to find a solution to it. Some New Age ideologies, for example, say that suffering is a mirage, an illusion we dream up for ourselves or call down on ourselves by having the wrong attitude or psychology. The power of positive thinking could rescue us from every ill, they claim. And the overarching power of negative thinking could destroy all of creation if we allow it.

Buddhism locates the source of suffering in "attachment," our valuing of people and things that are passing. When we are attached to possessions, our health, famiy and friends, or the way things are, we will certainly suffer, because none of these are permanent. The holy way is outlined as practicing detachment—we cling to nothing, expect nothing, and find peace in all things.

Judaism, like many of its ancient neighbors' religions, understands suffering to be a direct result of sin. The relationship of human suffering to the choice for evil is explained in the Genesis myth of the Garden. Disobeying God's law leads to painful consequences for all of creation. Obeying God's law leads to the fullness of God's blessings.

The problem of innocent suffering persisted, however, long after the rabbis and Wisdom writers first outlined this understanding. So later writers created additions to the theology. Some innocent sufferers would likely be victims of the choices others made to do evil. These innocents would know the fullness of God's blessings after death, in a time reserved for God's justice.

Despite all of this, the idea that suffering and sin are related persists in the religious imagination. In the time of Jesus, the poor, the sick, and the physically and mentally disabled are judged to be sinners or possessed by demons. If they were righteous, they would not have come to misfortune. The question is put to Jesus concerning the man born blind: "Who sinned, this man or his parents, that he was born blind?" In the wide-eyed innocence of this question, we hear the absolute conviction that someone's sin led to this punishment. If everything we understand about God is true, then human failure is the source of its own pain.

What we understand to be true about God, of course, is very often the point of total system failure for our theologies. This is clear in the story of the folktale character called Job. The Book of Job in the Hebrew scriptures is really a treatise on human suffering and how imperfectly religious answers meet the question. Job's wife, bitter with the sudden series of misfortunes, decides that God is unfair. That is what suffering is about: God's cruel injustice and nothing more. "Curse God, and die," she insists. Job's religious-minded friends come in with a set of religious prejudices of their own, presuming Job is a dreadful sinner. Now, they know him well enough to see that he is apparently a good man, a faithful believer. But since they have already decided that suffering is the direct result of sin, they have to question their experience of him as a good man. He must have committed some vile and secret sin for which God is tormenting him.

Job is left with a difficult choice. He knows he is innocent, and believes God is just. He is also horribly convinced that his suffering is no mirage. He cannot knit the threads of his experience and his knowledge of God together. They contradict and make no sense. So he does the only two things that a faithful sufferer can do: he laments, long and loud and deep. And he demands an audience with God. He wants God to explain what he alone cannot comprehend.

When Job encounters the Voice from the Whirlwind, he finds himself entirely vindicated. As Job says so bravely, "I know that my Redeemer lives," and his faith is answered. The friends of Job are rebuked by God for not having spoken "what is right" about the Almighty, as Job had. The crime of the friends is entered into scripture for all time: they are guilty of Bad Theology.

We want to know why we suffer. We want to be assured God is real and God is just. And we want our suffering to have meaning.

But why did Job suffer? God defends Job's innocence but does not give an answer to the central question. God defends the divine prerogative to do anything and everything in a long and eloquent passage about the wonder and genius of creation. But does that mean God can afflict or permit suffering for divine reasons that we are too finite to understand?

Ultimately, we want many things answered here. We want to know why we suffer. We want to be assured God is real and God is just. And we want our suffering to have meaning. It is bad enough to feel pain, worse if the pain is useless and senseless.

Archibald MacLeish, in his play about Job called *J.B.*, has the devil character speak our dilemma for us:

If God is God, He is not good;
If God is good, He is not God.

If God is all-powerful, then God could prevent suffering. And if God is all-good, God would want to prevent suffering. So the presence of suffering causes us to question either God's omnipotence or nature. Is it that God can't stop human suffering, or that God doesn't care enough to stop it? Is suffering ultimately our fault because of sin, or God's fault because of negligence?

People who believe that suffering is ultimately God's fault make peculiar disciples. They worship a God who is basically less moral than they are. Yet many people who are faithful churchgoers fall into this camp. Either fear or resignation seems to motivate them to faith. They tend to say of painful circumstances, "I guess it's God's will," and a very dark will they attribute to God at that, piling up cancers, accidents, lost jobs, and miscarriages at heaven's door. In this sense, they are not unlike Job's friends who are convicted of the crime of Bad Theology. How can a lively faith emerge from such a monstrous image of God?

On the other hand, people who see suffering as basically humanity's fault have a dark image of themselves. God may be "redeemed" in this understanding, but we humans are lost. We cause a world full of trouble, from earthquakes and diseases to droughts and infertility. We must be very, very bad to live in such a world.

What's worse is that the few good people who exist alongside us are punished by our pollutions and pestilence just the same. Original sin has been twisted to include a kind of backhand logic about this: if you didn't actually sin yourself, your ancestors did, so you carry the guilt by association.

When Jesus is confronted with the question, "Who sinned, this man or his parents?", he looks coolly past the sin-suffering connection and says, "Neither." In one word, Jesus explodes the sin-suffering bridge and tells us, essentially, that we don't "get" God at all. We look at suffering and try to assess blame. Jesus says the man born blind carries his affliction for God's glory.

So what happens if we look to suffering for signs of God's glory? A man in a wheelchair makes his way up the street, his body withered and twisted like a pretzel. One outstretched arm bent in three directions guides the advance of the chair. His face twitches with palsy, and most onlookers turn their faces as he goes by, not wanting to stare, afraid to see too much of his suffering. But out of the crowd steps a woman who smiles. Maybe it's a smile of mercy or charity; maybe it's just a smile that fellow human beings exchange on the street. At the sight of a friendly face, the man in the chair responds with a grin so huge, spreading crookedly over his features, that it shines over the woman, the crowd, and pours into the street like a shower of golden light.

"I have seen the Lord!" someone in the crowd

murmurs. Indeed. To recognize the real humanity of those who suffer is also to be open to the encounter with real divinity as well. Is there a window open so wide on the Kingdom as the window on a humanity deeply lived? And do we encounter the depth of our humanity anywhere so completely as in the well of suffering?

Jesus told us not to look for him in palaces and fine places but in the least of our brothers and sisters. We won't find Jesus at tables groaning with food or in the faces of powerful people. Those who serve the lowly ones are full of stories of finding Jesus in the dirty child, the man with AIDS, the mentally retarded woman. Those who work in the care of the dying see the glory of God revealed in the transparent last days of a person's life.

Jesus responds to suffering people with great respect, valuing their lives and affirming God's compassion for them. When he challenges the sin-suffering connection, he goes beyond the revelation of Job. Job was told that the mystery of suffering is for God alone to fathom. Jesus tells us that God will make use of our suffering, even bring it to fulfillment in glory and transformation.

And Jesus goes far beyond Job and all other prophets, wisdom, and theologies when he ascends the cross. Christianity responds to the problem of suffering in a wonder-filled way. The revelation of Jesus is that God is indeed loving and good and has power to do all things. Yet with all that love and all that goodness, God chooses to descend into our suffering, all the way to the end. If God's glory is revealed in the curing of the man born blind, how much more can we discover it in the life beyond the cross.

But to know that God shares in our suffering and is present with us in our pain does not tell us *why* we suffer. Knowing that God can bring glory out of human weakness gives it meaning and gives us hope, but it is not a direct answer to the question, *Why?* Even Jesus, in the midst of great anguish, raises the question, *Why have you forsaken me?* He trusts in God's attention, or he wouldn't spend his last breath in this prayer. He trusts in God's goodness, or he would not have obediently surrendered to the mission that led to the cross. But his faith and his obedience do not keep him from shouting out the question that tears through the soul of every sufferer, *Why?*

*K*nowing that God can bring glory out of human weakness gives it meaning and gives us hope, but it is not a direct answer to the question, Why?

Because Jesus asks it from the cross, we can be sure it's a legitimate question and a profoundly human one. And if Job is defended by God but never satisfied with a reply, Jesus is risen to new life but just as surely forfeits the old one in the silence that surrounds his final question.

Twice before in the gospels, Jesus hears a voice from heaven say, "This is my Son, the Beloved son, with whom I am well pleased." God does not reply from heaven while Jesus is dying, perhaps because a truly mortal death is not accompanied by assurances. Our suffering is surrounded by a sacred silence. Even the Son of God receives no word of reply.

What we can do is study Psalm 22 as the final testament of Jesus to those whom he taught to pray. Jesus chose to cry out his anguish with this psalm, rather than another. Within it are not only tones of agony but also absolute faith in deliverance. We can make it our prayer in times of pain and loss, now and at the hour of our death. Nowhere else can we find a more honest expression of our need for God:

> Yet it was you who took me from the womb;
>> you kept me safe on my mother's breast.

> On you I was cast from my birth,
>> and since my mother bore me
>> you have been my God.

> Do not be far from me,
>> for trouble is near
>> and there is no one to help.

THE FIFTH WORD

I am thirsty.

THE FIFTH WORD

When the soldiers had crucified Jesus, they took his clothes and divided them into four parts, one for each soldier. They also took his tunic; now the tunic was seamless, woven in one piece from the top. So they said to one another, "Let us not tear it, but cast lots for it to see who will get it." This was to fulfill what the scripture says,

> *"They divided my clothes among themselves,*
> *and for my clothing they cast lots."*

After this, when Jesus knew that all was now finished, he said (in order to fulfill the scripture), "I AM THIRSTY" (John 19:23-24, 28).

THIRST

"ARE YOU able to drink the cup that I am about to drink?" Jesus asks this question of James and John before the final entry into Jerusalem. The two young men were sure that they should sit in the places of honor when he came into his reign in the city of kings. James and John were ready for Jerusalem: pomp, splendor, riches, leadership. Imagine, two local boys from Galilee going all the way to the top!

And why not these two, after all? Whenever Jesus chose among the Twelve, it was Peter and these brothers who accompanied him. The special three were with him at the Transfiguration, and would be with him in the Garden of Gethsemane. Peter, James, and John had precedence among the disciples.

Only two, of course, were needed to sit on either side of Jesus. James and John wanted to get their bids in early.

It was a snub against the other disciples, who voiced their protest immediately. But Jesus was not indignant at the request. In fact, he seems quieted by it, maybe saddened and amused at the same time. "You do not know what you are asking," he explains. That was an understatement. What awaited Jesus in Jerusalem was a fate none of them seemed to grasp, though he had warned them many times that he was going to his death. In fact, when it came time for Jesus to be lifted up in Jerusalem, two strangers would take their places at his right and at his left.

"Are you able to drink the cup?" he asks them, knowing they cannot imagine that what fills it is his blood. With confidence, they say, "We are able."

Jesus assures them that they will, that what awaits them is what awaits all who will follow after him with a single heart. So what is this cup, from which we are all asked to drink? When we boldly answer, "We are able," and drink the blessing cup of the Eucharist, what fate are we agreeing to share?

Drinking from the cup is an ancient ritual of sharing in the fortune of a benefactor. The head of the household filled the cups of the guests personally, giving them

a share in his bounty. The cup itself comes to symbolize
the allotted portion one receives from the person in
power. Since cups were also used for divining the will of
the gods in the ancient world (see the story of Joseph in
Genesis), one's personal cup represented a certain
authority in itself. We only need think of the practice of
reading tea leaves to get a sense of what it means to look
to the cup for a sign of one's destiny. We still share a
drink with friends to celebrate a triumph, so we understand the metaphor of sharing our bounty in the sharing
of the cup.

But the allotted portion and cup could also brim
with misfortune. The cup of God's wrath is poured out on
God's enemies, as in the Book of Revelation, or forced
into the hands of the wicked, as in Psalm 75:

> For in the hand of the Lord's is a cup
>   with foaming wine, well mixed;
> he will pour a draught from it;
>   and all the wicked of the earth
>   shall drain it down to the dregs.

Being invited to drink from the cup was no guaran-
tee of well-being. But in Israel, the allotted cup most of
all came to symbolize God's will and destiny for the
people. The people even prayed in Psalm 16, "The Lord is
my chosen portion and my cup," meaning that the
destiny of Israel is bound to the will of God.

Jesus asks his disciples if they can accept a portion
of his destiny in Jerusalem, and they say they can. And we
know, when the time comes, they cannot. But Jesus
knows that they answer not just for the coming week but

for the long haul and that, sooner or later, most of the
disciples will share his destiny in martyrdom.

But first, Jesus must drink from the cup himself, and
it is no simple matter. In the Garden, he prays that his
Father may take the cup away from him. In the second
repetition in Matthew's version, he prays, "My Father, if
this cannot pass unless I drink it, your will be done."
Unlike the disciples who are willing to drink the portion
they do not understand, Jesus does appreciate the destiny
that is contained in the Father's will. And it is not a
destiny he desires to take on, unless it will serve God for
him to do it.

And now, fixed to the cross, watching the men
callously divide his earthly goods while he dies, Jesus
says, *I am thirsty.* It is a natural thing that he should
thirst, after a night of trials and beatings, a torturous walk
to the hill, and the noonday heat drawing the sweat from
his body. We have no reason to doubt his need for water.

And yet, in John's gospel nothing is ever as simple as
it appears. Once before in this gospel Jesus spoke of
thirst, in the noonday heat of Samaria. On that occasion,
after a long journey through desert lands, it was plausible
for Jesus to want water. But when he asks a Samaritan
woman for a drink, the ensuing conversation becomes so
much more than a request made out of mortal thirst.
The promise of living water becomes more compelling
than any thirst born of sun and sand. The woman
abandons her water jar at the well, and as far as we
know, Jesus never gets a drink. The water of earth loses
its appeal in the sufficiency of the living water of Spirit.

When the disciples return from town with food that

afternoon, Jesus does not eat. He explains to his friends, "My food is to do the will of him who sent me and to complete his work." The food and drink of the world is never what interests Jesus. Even when he sits at the table of his last supper, he imbues the humble elements of common food with new meaning and a spiritual dimension.

When Jesus says from the cross, *I am thirsty*, we can be sure his heart is not fixed on water from a well or wine from a jug. Jesus thirsts for the living water of his Father's will, to drink from the cup that God is holding out to him. At the end, he is ready to receive his allotted portion as the Son of Love.

Can we drink from the cup that is held out for those who follow Jesus?

When Jesus says from the cross, "I am thirsty," we can be sure his heart is not fixed on water from a well or wine from a jug. Jesus thirsts for the living water of his Father's will.

When we receive the cup of the Lord's blood in the Eucharist, we share our allotted portion with one another, accepting only a taste from the cup. Yet that alone is solemn enough, for we signal our willingness to share in the cup of Christ's Passion to do his Father's will—no matter what the cost.

Still, we are not asked to do this alone but through the power of the Spirit. In Mark's gospel, Jesus phrases his question to the sons of Zebedee this way: "Are you able to drink the cup that I drink, or be baptized with the baptism that I am baptized with?" Jesus is referring to the "baptism by fire" that awaits him in Jerusalem, but both baptism and fire are words related to the activity of the Holy Spirit. As Jesus says elsewhere in Luke, "I came to bring fire to the earth, and how I wish it were already kindled! There is a baptism with which I must be baptized, and how great is my anguish until it is accomplished!"

With the image of baptism, we come full circle to water again, and our thirst for a water that wells up to life everlasting. Jesus equates the fire he has come to kindle with his Passion on the cross, and that fire is the Kingdom itself. All heaven breaks loose like a forest fire from the cross, and the Holy Spirit is in the heart of the flames. When we share Christ's cup and his baptism, we become heirs to the Kingdom and companions of the Spirit. The fire of the Kingdom rages on in us.

We who share the life of the cup have a thirst that marks us. We hunger and thirst for righteousness, as the Beatitude says, and we will be filled. *Righteousness,* or justice, comes from the same Hebrew root meaning "right relationship." Hebrew justice doesn't mean simply doing things fairly but rather giving to each what is due to each. As Jesus pointed out, what we owe to Caesar is different from what we owe to God. When we are in right relationship with God, our neighbor, our enemy, and the stranger, then we are living in justice. We who share the life of the cup cannot be satisfied until those relationships are at peace.

Our thirst compels us to look to our stewardship of

creation and to be concerned with the crises of our environment. Part of right relationship with the Creator is to tend the garden we have been given–the planet as a whole–and all of its lesser creatures. A just relationship with God also entails reverence in worship, attentiveness to prayer, obedient listening to the Spirit within, and a grateful heart. Appreciating the beauty of the world is a sacred obligation we often fail to acknowledge. Living gratefully is one way to fulfill Saint Paul's injunction to "pray unceasingly."

Our thirst for justice means caring for our neighbor, who is by biblical definition both friend and stranger alike. Even hypocrites will do favors for those who will return them, Jesus reminds us. Therefore giving to our friends what is due in friendship is only the beginning of living in right relationship with our neighbor. Our thirst leads us to comfort the afflicted stranger, to become involved in circumstances that are none of our business. We are called to step into situations, personal and political, that are guaranteed to be messy, uncomfortable, and perhaps costly to us. Justice is not a mere matter for the courts, not something in which we can involve ourselves at arm's length. The Good Samaritan has become a metaphor for do-gooding, but the story is really about a man taking his life in his hands by stopping to care for the welfare of his enemy.

Which brings us to justice and our proper relation-ship to our enemy. Jesus said it simply when he told us to love our enemies. This is perhaps the greatest risk we take in our thirst for justice, but it is the one that may do us the most good. As the Son of Love, Jesus had to unite

himself to love in every way. He forgave his enemies from
the cross and left this world with an undivided heart,
restoring peace between God and Creation. So long as we
divide the world into friends and enemies, we live with
division in our hearts and cannot know the perfect love
that we share as our allotted portion.

Loving our enemies begins with forgiveness. We must
forgive ourselves, our original families, our present communities, our co-workers, our leaders, and anyone we are
tempted to fear, hate, or blame. In forgiving those who
have wronged us in the past or continue to thwart us in
the present, we prepare a place for healing to come and
peace to dwell. Without these measures—forgiveness,
healing, and peace—we cannot share in the joy of the
Kingdom. So the injunction to love our enemies is not just
for our enemies' sake but for our own. In loving those we
are drawn to hate, we give the darkness no foothold in our
lives, the devil has no victory, and death has no sting.

I am thirsty, Jesus says, and in his thirst the scriptures
are fulfilled. He drinks deeply of the cup of his Father's
will, and the Kingdom is poured out like a baptism of fire.
When we drink deeply from the same cup, we experience
the fire of Spirit and the living water that has no end. Our
love will know no boundaries. Our lives will blaze like
pillars in the darkness, guiding others to the heart of God.

THE SIXTH WORD

It is finished.

THE SIXTH WORD

When Jesus had received the wine, he said, "IT IS FINISHED" (John 19:30).

THE CROSS

WE HUMANS have a deep distrust of endings. Something in the human spirit answers every farewell with a resounding No! We prefer not to say good-bye but rather "see you later." We turn graduations into commencements, wanting to respond to endings with beginnings. We do everything we can to promote continuance, to avoid the near occasion of closure.

Maybe we learn to suspend our belief in endings from the earth, from seasons that turn and are enfolded into the next. We observe the cycles of life in nature and see each death as preparation for a new season of life and growth. Nature gathers up the fragments of the old that nothing may be wasted. All is made new out of the weavings of decay.

Every spiritual path seeks to respond to the innate disbelief in a personal ending. Death is seen as a moment of transition from life as we know it to something more. Belief in reincarnation, the translation from material life to pure spirit, or the Christian understanding of resurrection, body and spirit, are all ways of expressing our rejection of a personal end. The expression "life goes on" is not simply a cliché but more like a secular creed. What we hope to mean is: "I will go on."

When relationships are broken or loved ones are lost to death, we feel both the loss and the nonrational certainty that, in a real sense, nothing is lost and the relationship continues. Something may come to an end objectively out there, but subjectively within us, nothing ever really ends. People we haven't seen for years still communicate their love and support—or disapproval—inside of us. Situations that are long ended continue to heal or haunt us. The idea that anything really dies forever is alien to our experience.

The great Christian story tells us that when Jesus says, *It is finished,* he is not saying that he is finished, or that anything is lost in his dying. In fact, the opposite is true. So much is begun on the cross, and so much is gained, that these words about endings are entirely about triumph and not at all about defeat.

This wasn't clear to those who surrounded Jesus that final week of his life. Caiaphas and the other religious leaders convened the Sanhedrin to discuss the Jesus Problem, and they decided that putting him to death would be the perfect solution. Once Jesus was killed, his disciples would disperse and the unpleasant challenges to Temple and Torah authority would end. The political tension of having too many restless citizens gathering in the streets of an occupied country would be eased. There would be no trouble from the Romans, and once again there could be business as usual in Jerusalem. It would all be finished once Jesus was executed, and his little religious cult would vanish from the earth.

Pilate, too, was concerned about getting back to business as usual. More specifically, he wanted this unpleasant mock trial of an innocent man to be done with. His wife had had a disturbing dream, and Pilate was reluctant to proceed with the otherwise routine solution of capital punishment. Besides, the man himself was disturbing to behold. He looked like any other poor Jewish wretch after suffering a sound lashing and the cruelty of the guards. Yet he had a regal air about him that was more than delusional. He really did seem more like a king than all the royalty of Judea put together. He had an authority about him that made Pilate feel somehow small and inadequate. Pilate didn't like the way the whole thing wound up, having his hand forced by the local leadership, as if he weren't the procurator of the land. But at least it was finished, and he could forget about it. The sooner he could disassociate his name from the man from Galilee, the better.

Peter and the disciples, huddled together in the upper room, prayed for it all to be over soon. For the sake of the man they loved and had followed, they wanted this dark day to end. They wanted his misery to be short, for God to show some mercy on a holy and innocent man. They also, quite naturally, wanted the public scandal to blow over quickly, so they could creep out of the city and back to Galilee where they belonged. The sea looked better to them every moment since the tide turned against them in Jerusalem. They longed for the old life, for their wives and the predictable work of their hands. They wanted to forget they had ever dreamed of kingdoms and justice. There was no justice. Justice had been nailed to a cross, and all they had left were shreds of teachings that seemed like fool's gold now. Maybe God took care of the lilies, but not of the one who had called God Father. The life of that one, and all the hopes his life had raised, were finished.

The women gathered under the cross were broken-hearted. Love was dying above them, and they were helpless to stop it or even ease the pain. Jesus had given them such comfort, forgiveness, healing, and hope, and they could give him nothing in this hour. All they could do was be present to his suffering and not look away. It was a poor offering, a widow's mite. They watched and wept and wrung their hands. They saw his agony go on, his breath labored, his bruises darkening, the blood mixing with sweat on his bare flesh. They heard his final words: a short conversation with a dying convict, a prayer cried out to God, a few words to his mother and the one disciple who dared to stay. He forgave those who were murdering him—they would never forget that as long as they lived! And he had asked for water—or was it water he was asking for? His gaze seemed to be on something farther than they could see. And now he said: *It is finished.* They looked up, but they could see he didn't mean his dying at all. His chin was high, and he seemed confident, ready, almost serene. As astonishing as it seems, it was as if he had intended the cross, as though it were but one more thing that served his purposes, like the mud he used for healing eyes or the demons he cast out of the possessed. What was finished? His mission?

And Jesus, after he had tasted the wine, said: *It is finished. It is perfected. It is accomplished. It is consummated!* His words would be translated in all these ways and more through the centuries, as people sought to understand them. To the writer John, Jesus was the Divine Christ from before time, the Word who was with God before the creation of the world. Jesus was always in control of his destiny, a destiny ordained by God and not made by human hands. "For this reason the Father loves me," he once told his disciples, "because I lay down my life in order to take it up again. No one takes it from me, but I lay it down of my own accord. I have power to lay it down, and I have power to take it up again." God chooses the hour, Jesus assured his followers. Jesus himself chose the surrender.

This exit at the cross was no accident . . . but the brave course that Love took to empty divinity into humanity and humanity into death itself.

When Jesus says, *It is finished,* he closes his mission on earth by laying down his life. It is no helpless surrender, but a deliberate action, freely chosen. Even from the cross, the Divine Word has the power to create reality. The power of the Word once made light, time, and world come into being. Now that same Word calls the earthly mission to an end, names the hour, and enters into glory.

The mission is not only ended, but perfected. This

exit at the cross was no accident or mere tragedy but the brave course that Love took to empty divinity into humanity and humanity into death itself. The raising up of that same person into glory would have meaning for all of us who must go by way of death from this world. The Word became flesh to travel the way of all flesh. And now we who are flesh can surrender ourselves to death with confidence.

Something is accomplished, too, in the mission that led Jesus to the cross. The Father's will is done, on earth as perfectly as in heaven. Love chose to testify to the truth, without compromise. Love chose fidelity over self-preservation, the beloved over the self. The Kingdom has been announced, and its arrival is at hand, awaiting only our willingness to receive it.

Perhaps the most meaningful translation of this phrase is the lover's cry: *It is consummated!* It speaks of love reaching its fullness. It reminds us that heaven and earth are reconciled as of old, the ancient enmity bridged at last. The two are made one: God and flesh at table. To see the union of love transposed upon the loneliness of the cross is to understand Transfiguration at its deepest level. The glory is hidden in the humility. Life waits in the darkness of the tomb. Love bursts forth unseen in the moment of apparent abandonment.

In the words of Jesus, we come to understand that everything he intended by his mission is completed, and nothing he has started will come to an end. "And remember, I am with you always, to the end of the age," Jesus guarantees his followers. This means that those who contemplated his death were quite mistaken about it.

The religious leaders hoped to finish off his following, yet for 20 centuries it has extended to all the world. Pilate hoped to wash himself clean of the disturbing association, and yet his name is forever linked to the cross in our creed. The disciples wanted to forget that terrible Friday, but they would instead spend their lives and go to their deaths proclaiming it. The women believed that Love was dying with Jesus, not realizing that Love is stronger than death.

The unchallenged reign of sin is ended, the fatal sting of death is vanquished. The mission of Jesus has been satisfied, but like so many apparent endings, the pronouncement *It is finished* is more about beginnings. The cross did not finish Jesus, and death can never make an end of us. The church began in the blood and water that poured from Jesus' heart, early writers insisted. We owe our mission to the completion of that fateful hour.

The cross was a good and faithful servant that Jesus chose to use in the service of the One who sent him. The cross continues to serve us in our mission as church. It is the sign with which we mark ourselves, our buildings, our worship, our tombstones. It is the sign of membership in baptism, and the sign of blessing throughout our lives. We say it is the sign under which we are saved, the sign that teaches us our true identity. *In the name of the Father, and of the Son, and of the Holy Spirit*–so we begin and end our every prayer. Through the Creator, we understand our creatureliness, our dependence on the Source of life. Through the Redeemer, we know that God does not abandon us even as we pass through the portal of death. Through the Sanctifier, we bless our world, seeking holiness in our work, our relationships, our very being. The cross is our greatest teacher. What makes us Christian is our willingness to face it and even to bear it for one another.

The cross is, very literally, a crossroads. The vertical and horizontal dimensions are the intersection of divinity and humanity, death and life, endings and beginnings, humiliation and glory. It was meant to be an instrument of execution, but it became the source of salvation for all. An act of cruelty was transformed into utter generosity and compassion. This is the meaning of the cross: that any low or base motive can be lifted up through the power of the cross and become a conduit for grace. We "offer up" what sin brings into our lives and ask that it be taken and blessed, broken and shared, no longer the poison of our souls but the food of goodness and truth. Through the power of the cross, every force that threatens to harm us must surrender to the transformation of grace. We are saved, which is another way of saying we are safe.

It is finished. Yet it also *begins* here at the cross, a life without end. We who are privileged to bear this sign should contemplate it often. It reminds us that, no matter what sin does, love does more.

THE SEVENTH WORD

Father, into your hands
I commend my spirit.

THE SEVENTH WORD

It was now about noon, and darkness came over the whole land until three in the afternoon, while the sun's light failed; and the curtain of the temple was torn in two. Then Jesus crying with a loud voice said, "FATHER, INTO YOUR HANDS I COMMEND MY SPIRIT" (Luke 23:44-46).

SURRENDER

AND SO JESUS breathes his last. The old Catholic Douay translation reads, "Jesus gave up the ghost." What the earlier translation may lack in accuracy, it does make up for in soul. "Giving up the ghost" signals surrender. The strife is over, the battle done, as the old hymn goes.

The thought of surrender is morbid for many of us. It means defeat, failure, weakness, loss. When the white flag goes up, all we've got to hope for is mercy. And that's mercy from our enemies, no less. Surrender is the choice of last resort. It is the fate all of us hope to avoid.

So we enter into the battleground of life with our shields raised. We protect ourselves by building up bigger and better interior defenses to keep our hearts safe. We acquire as much wealth as we can to be secure. We garner prestige and power to stand on top or ahead of others, so as not to fall behind and be crushed by everyone else who is scrambling up the ladders of success. We gather things around ourselves to help us to relax, and then we have to work twice as hard to maintain our amusements. "The more we have, the more we have to protect," Franciscan priest Richard Rohr reminds us. The machinery of our armor grows heavier as the years advance. The attacks on our security come from all sides: family disappoints us, friends fail us, companions betray us, our health weakens, a job is suddenly lost, property is stolen or ravaged by nature, an investment goes bad. We continue to fortify our defense, adding to our stockpile of weapons and rebuttals. We must not lose. We will not surrender. We color our hair, have surgeries to reconstruct our youth, and keep pretending as long as we can that we are the masters of our own fates.

And, in the peculiar paradox of the Kingdom, the one thing we most hope to avoid is the very thing we are called upon to do. As impossible as it seems to us, "power is made perfect in weakness," Saint Paul reminds us. "For whenever I am weak, then I am strong." Paul wants to persuade us that human strength stands in the way of the power of Christ, which seeks a home in us. So all of our attempts to save ourselves with money and power and illusions of vigor are in vain. All of these will fall away and reveal themselves as lies, as the offspring of the Father of Lies. It took an angel of Satan, Saint Paul says, to plague him with beatings before he "got" it—that his self-defense was making him weaker and not stronger. Elsewhere Jesus says, "Offer no resistance to an evildoer." We cannot hope to fight and conquer evil, so to pit ourselves against it ties up all of our energy in a losing battle. What is better is to put ourselves at the service of God and good. This is a lesson the world has not yet learned.

The gentle answer to the threats and troubles of human existence is to surrender. This counters Darwin and the notion of the survival of the fittest, but the war of evolution is not the one we as Christians hope to win. We are disciples of the Lord of Surrender, who did not grasp at equality with God, but took the form of the servant instead. We follow the master who washed the feet of his students. We follow the teacher who said we should seek the lowest place at the table and serve the least of our sisters and brothers. Winning anything that the world values is not the goal for us. So we have nothing to fear from surrender. Still we resist. What if we should pray as Jesus did, *Father, into your hands I commend my spirit?* What if we, too, gave up the ghost of our personal successes and placed ourselves in God's hands? What would happen to us? The answer has to be: nothing we have imagined; everything we can dream of.

We can understand more about the nature of the Christian call to surrender by looking into this final word from the cross. The prayer that Jesus prays here is not original. Like the earlier word, *Why have you forsaken me?*, this one is from a Hebrew prayer for deliverance, Psalm 31. The whole psalm is worth reading to understand the context, but an excerpt here is useful:

> Be a rock of refuge for me,
>> a strong fortress to save me.
> You are indeed my rock and my fortress;
>> for your name's sake lead me and guide me.
> Take me out of the net that is hidden for me,
>> for you are my refuge.
> Into your hand I commit my spirit;
>> you will redeem me, O Lord, faithful God.

Jesus adds the word *Father* to the psalm, and that is important. In the fourth of the Seven Last Words, from Psalm 22, God is addressed from the depths of anguish, far away: *My God, my God.* In this Seventh Word, from Luke's gospel, Jesus lifts up a final prayer to the One he has always known as Father, the One who calls him beloved and has prepared a place for him.

There is a tender intimacy in this surrender into God's hands. Jesus doesn't simply give up the ghost but places himself in the hands of One who cares and awaits him. He doesn't simply die and go off into the void; he is *received.* The confidence and security Jesus displays is an incredible act of faith. We see that the fear he felt in the Garden has been resolved, replaced by the courage born of trust in God's will.

Jesus relinquishes his spirit, the same spirit that was given to him at the start of his ministry. What comes from the Father returns to the Father, simply and without clinging. Jesus knows how to give to God what is God's, a perfect act of justice.

That is one clarifying idea to keep in mind when pondering Christian surrender. We aren't about to lose anything that is truly ours. All we have is gift or, better yet, on loan. Like the steward who is given his master's talents to invest for his return, we can claim only a stewardship of our years and our abilities. To surrender ourselves to God's purposes is not to do God a favor but to seek God's guidance in our investments.

A second point to keep in mind is that, in the battleground of existence, surrender to God is not losing but winning. As Psalm 31 suggests, with God as a fortress, who needs self-defense? This kind of surrender is not slavery but the only real freedom there is. We are free *Jesus relinquishes his spirit, the same spirit that was given to him at the start of his ministry. What comes from the Father returns to the Father, simply and without clinging.*

from the rat race, from keeping up with the Joneses, from game-playing and trying to keep our deceptions consistent. We are free to tell the truth, live the truth, and hear the truth from others. We have nothing to hide and nothing to protect. What a relief!

When we have done well, we can witness to justice. When we have done badly, we can confess our guilt and be forgiven. The surrender Jesus teaches is not only a tremendous advantage; it is the only real sanity.

Father, into your hands I commend my spirit. In exchange for the surrender of our will, we receive the companion Jesus promised, the One who will be with us always to the end of time. The Holy Spirit of God will dwell in us. And that's some trade-off.

The exchange of spirits is a core reality of the Christian story. Jesus told his disciples that if he did not go to the Father, the Spirit could not come to them. The coming of the Spirit was vital, as Jesus himself did not do anything without its companionship. He was conceived by its power, baptized into its activity, and guided by its wisdom throughout his ministry.

Charismatic Catholics and Pentecostal Protestants speak of a very tangible experience of the Holy Spirit, but for many others, the Holy Spirit is the shadowiest member of the Trinity. We can understand God as Creator by looking at the world. We can come to know Jesus through his story, his teachings, and his great act of love on the cross. But when we try to apprehend the Holy Spirit, we find ourselves clutching air. The Holy Spirit is the Divine Actor without a face, the One who does not leave perceptible footprints.

Part of our problem is a catechetical one. Children were (maybe still are) taught about the Holy Spirit as kind of the Divine Big Bird, which is too odd a concept to carry over into adult faith. In parochial schools, many of us were instructed to pray to the Holy Spirit before taking tests, so we wound up in a functional relationship with this aspect of the Trinity as the great Answer-Bearer in the Sky. The scene in the upper room at Pentecost helps us get a better focus on the Spirit: the flame image ties in with God's earlier appearances in a burning bush and a smoking brazier in the Hebrew scriptures. Instead of raining down destructive fire and brimstone, however, the Holy Spirit descends as tongues of fire that alight on the disciples without harming them. We hear echoes of the Emmaus journey, "Were not our hearts burning within us while he was talking to us on the road?" The fire image helps us to comprehend the Spirit as divinity and power and passion, all at once.

But the Spirit is more than a being to be imagined. The Holy Spirit of God is more a verb than a noun, the very activity of God in the world. We often reduce the Spirit to lists of gifts and fruits–Saint Paul meant well, but his categories ended up as facts to be memorized by Confirmation classes, too static to breathe. And it is breath as much as fire that helps us to "get" the Spirit. The Hebrew word for spirit, *ruah*, means "air," "wind," or "breath." It is the substance of life, which God breathed into the first people. It was breathed upon the prophets to give them leave to speak as God's messengers. It was the small still voice that Elijah listened for, through storms and earthquakes, waiting for the authentic voice of God to speak to him.

Jesus commissions his disciples in the same way: "He breathed on them and said to them, 'Receive the Holy Spirit.'" This breath of God transmits the authority of Jesus–the guidance, wisdom, and power that animated him–to his disciples. And we are heirs of that same Holy Breath.

And what happens to us if we surrender our spirit and are taken up by the Spirit of God? The early Christian writers help to enlighten and also frighten us with their portrayal. Sometimes individuals and sometimes whole communities are swept up in the Spirit and begin praying in inspired speech and testifying to God's works. That part scares us, because it sounds like a total loss of self-control and good order. And, in fact, it sometimes led to both, which made Saint Paul have to play Bad Cop to the churches, telling them that chaos was not the goal of the Spirit's visitation. It also led to people selling off all of their goods and casting their fate into a common purse and table. That scares us worse. We are, at the deepest level of our beings, capitalists. Nobody's going to get our purse!

When it comes right down to it, the example of the early church convinces us that we definitely don't want to surrender to the Holy Spirit. It's too dangerous, too disruptive, too untidy!

When it comes right down to it, the example of the early church convinces us that we definitely *don't* want to surrender to the Holy Spirit. It's too dangerous, too disruptive, too untidy! We like the approach of the old Arab proverb "Trust in God, but tie your camel." Let's not get too carried away by this religion business! After all, we're not fanatics. We're Christians, good citizens, and

nice people to boot. We want a reasonable amount of
religion in our lives, just enough to give us a moral
compass and a place to worship on Sundays. We'd prefer
the orderly, if somewhat Pharisaic, approach to salvation:
do good deeds, pray regularly, and win God's approval the
old-fashioned way.

After all, look at what happens to people who get
carried away with the surrender thing: Francis and Clare,
Teresa of Avila, Cesar Chavez, archbishop Oscar Romero.
When you lose control of the enterprise of religion, the
next thing you know you're in the canon of saints. Forget
having a normal life, the American dream, and the
esteem of others. People who surrender to the overwhelming rush of God's breath in their lives end up
oddballs for the faith, people their own mothers wouldn't
recognize. They inspire young people to drop off the fast
track and enter their cosmic idealism. They move
mountains, some of which never get put back where they
belong. They change hearts, and they change history.
Sometimes they are loved, and sometimes they are killed.

Unless we are careful, we will end up losing our
hearts and going the same way. Tending to the gospel is
like playing with matches, and the fire of the Holy Spirit
may start when you least expect it. As the young prophet
Jeremiah laments of his encounter with God's word:

> Then within me there is something like a
>   burning fire
>   shut up in my bones;
> I am weary with holding it in,
>   and I cannot.

If we have no intention of changing our lives, then we can easily find a safe corner of religion and stay there. But those who find themselves compelled by the Seventh Word of Jesus may want to pray it often. And pray, too, the prayer that is a saint-maker, the words that dare God to make a saint of each of us:

Come, Holy Spirit,
fill the hearts of your faithful,
and kindle in them the fire of your love.
Send forth your Spirit and they will be created,
and you will renew the face of the earth.

Afterword

FOR TOO LONG popular piety has stressed our relationship to the cross as one of "how sad" or "what great love," leaving us in a sentimental morass that fuels our emotions without guiding us in how to respond, fully and completely, to this mystery. Many of us remember attending devotional evenings in which horror, pity, and guilt were the prominent features. While emotional attraction may lead to a desire to commit more fervently to a holy life, more often it has led simply to the next devotional service in which human sentiment could be again excited.

In the present generation of active, thoughtful lay involvement in the life of the church, sentimental religion won't do. It doesn't address the deeper issues in our lives, like how to live faithfully with a spouse, raise children, take care of the elderly, be responsive to the growing needs of the poor, maintain stewardship over the environment, make a just living, and balance allegiance to our country with fidelity to the Kingdom in our midst. Religious practices that encourage us in how to feel without assisting us in how to live are not only useless but perhaps harmful. Christian disciples need less introspective scrupulosity and more discernment to live out the gospel in a world that continues to harden its heart.

The Evangelists wrote the Passion accounts, not to point to the heroic nobility of the death of Jesus but to instruct the living community. Everything written in the gospels is intended for the instruction of new disciples, not as a commemoration of a life well lived. If we listen to the story of the crucifixion as a beautiful, moving history of the death of our Lord, we miss something crucial in the telling. What is Jesus inviting us to do? Is this a lesson in how to die or how to live?

The lessons of the cross are deceptively simple and not at all easy. We learn we are forgiven, why we are forgiven, and the proper response to this forgiveness. We recognize that we must understand the sovereignty of Jesus in his weakest hour and look for him in the suffering faces of our sisters and brothers. We come to understand that our call to be church is a call to acknowledge everyone, even the stranger and the enemy, as family. We begin to respect the sacred dimension of human suffering and believe that the One who will redeem us is alive. We tremble at the reception of our Eucharist, which binds us to the promise and the sacrifice of our Savior. We see the cross not as an end of life but the beginning of a life that will never end. We encounter death in a new way, not only its momentary sorrow but its eternal joy. We experience the seduction of a world that bids us to share its empty values and know we are to surrender ourselves only and completely to the Spirit of Holiness that harbors all truth and meaning.

Who will we be if we listen to the lessons of the Last Words of Jesus? People of love and joy, ready to forgive, buoyed by hope. We will honor our families, welcome the outsider, serve Christ in the needs of others. We will take our sacraments of commitment and healing and service seriously. We will stand with those who are suffering and be the presence of Christ for them. We will fight fear and despair, bringing the Good News of the Kingdom everywhere we go, especially where it is least understood. Again and again, we will surrender to the Holy Spirit of God so that it will be no longer we who live but Christ who lives in us.

The world is in such need of people like this. One holy person is worth all the sermons on holiness we might ever hear. If you have the courage to be that person, the Kingdom comes wherever you are.

About the Author

ALICE CAMILLE is a writer, religious educator, and storyteller. She received her Master of Divinity at the Franciscan School of Theology at Berkeley, where she currently teaches preaching and proclamation. She is the author of several commentaries on scripture and numerous articles on living faithfully and with passion.

Also Available from
ACTA Publications

**SEVEN LAST WORDS: LENTEN REFLECTIONS
FOR TODAY'S BELIEVERS,** an audio tape by ALICE CAMILLE.
This abridged text of Alice Camille's book *Seven Last Words* is
combined with choral and instrumental music to produce seven
Lenten meditations suitable for individual or group reflection.
(49 minutes, audio cassette, $9.95)

THE STATIONS OF THE CROSS, meditations by
REV. JAMES KILLGALLON; music by SHELDON COHEN.
Blending the spoken word and music, this tape is truly an
occasion of grace and prayerfulness. The video tape adds
magnificent visual images for each of the fourteen stations.
(40 minutes: audio cassette, $8.95; video tape, $19.95)

**PRAY TO LOVE, LOVE TO PRAY:
PRAYERS, REFLECTIONS, AND LIFE STORIES
OF 14 GREAT PRAY-ERS**
For each of the 14 saintly people portrayed in this book—from
Saint Augustine to Mother Teresa—there is a collection of that
individual's prayers and important sayings along with a brief
biographical sketch. (64 pages, paperback, $5.95)

**MORE PRAY TO LOVE, LOVE TO PRAY:
PRAYERS, REFLECTIONS, AND LIFE STORIES
OF 15 GREAT PRAY-ERS**
Prayers, sayings and a brief biography of 15 more great pray-ers,
from Saints Clare and Bernard to Archbishop Oscar Romero.
(64 pages, paperback, $5.95)

AVAILABLE FROM BOOKSELLERS OR CALL 800-397-2282